Celebrations!

Divali

Anita Ganeri

H www.heinemann.co.uk/library
Visit our website to find out more information about Heinemann Library books.

To order:
☎ Phone 44 (0) 1865 888066
🗎 Send a fax to 44 (0) 1865 314091
🖳 Visit the Heinemann Bookshop at www.heinemann.co.uk/library to browse our catalogue and order online.

First published in Great Britain by Heinemann Library,
Halley Court, Jordan Hill, Oxford OX2 8EJ
a division of Reed Educational and Professional Publishing Ltd.
Heinemann is a registered trademark of Reed Educational & Professional Publishing Ltd.

OXFORD MELBOURNE AUCKLAND
JOHANNESBURG BLANTYRE GABORONE
IBADAN PORTSMOUTH (NH) USA CHICAGO

© Reed Educational and Professional Publishing Ltd 2002
The moral right of the proprietor has been asserted.

Designed by Celia Floyd
Originated by Ambassador Litho Ltd
Printed by Wing King Tong in Hong Kong

ISBN 0 431 13793 5 (hardback)   ISBN 0 431 13801 X (paperback)
06 05 04 03 02   06 05 04 03 02
10 9 8 7 6 5 4 3 2   10 9 8 7 6 5 4 3 2 1

British Library Cataloguing in Publication Data

Ganeri, Anita
  Divali. – (Celebrations)
  1. Divali – Juvenile literature
  I. Title
  394.2'6545

Acknowledgements

The Publishers would like to thank the following for permission to reproduce photographs:
Andes Press Agency: Carlos Reyes-Manzo p14; Ann and Bury Peerless: pp6, 7; Christine Osborne Pictures: p12: Corbis: Tim Hawkins (Eye Ubiquitous) p4, Arvind Garg p8; Dinodia Picture Agency: p19, 20, Sudheer Babji p15; ffotograff: Patricia Aithie p18; Hutchison Library: Liba Taylor p5, Michael Macintyre p21; Judy Harrison/Format: p9; Sally Greenhill: p11: Sarah Thorley: p10; Trip: H Rogers pp13, 16, 17

Cover photograph reproduced with permission of Trip: A Tovy

Our thanks to the Bradford Interfaith Education Centre for their comments in the preparation of this book.

Every effort has been made to contact copyright holders of any material reproduced in this book. Any omissions will be rectified in subsequent printings if notice is given to the Publisher.

Contents

Words printed in **bold letters like these** are explained in the glossary.

Festival of lights

In October or November, **Hindus** celebrate the festival of Divali. This is a very happy time in the Hindu year. Divali is the Hindu festival of light. People decorate their homes with small lights, called **divas**. Strings of twinkling fairylights light up the streets. People send each other Divali cards and give gifts of sweets and new clothes.

A street decorated for Divali. The decoration shows that the name of the festival can be spelt differently.

Children lighting diva lamps for Divali.

There are many reasons for celebrating Divali. Some people remember the story of Prince Rama. Long ago, he defeated the evil demon, Ravana, and came home to be crowned king. People also **worship Lakshmi**, the goddess of wealth and good fortune. For some Hindus, Divali is the start of the new year. Wherever Divali is celebrated, its message is the same. It is a time for celebrating the triumph of good over evil and of hope for a happy future.

The story of Rama and Sita

At Divali, **Hindus** remember the story of Prince Rama. Long ago, King Dasaratha ruled a **kingdom** in north India. Prince Rama was his eldest son and the **heir** to his throne. But Rama's stepmother wanted her son, Prince Bharata, to be king instead. Rama was sent to live in the forest. He could not return home for many years. His wife, Sita, and his brother, Lakshman, went with him.

Rama, Sita and Lakshman in the forest.

One day, Rama and Lakshman were out hunting. While they were gone, a **holy** man came to Sita's door and begged her for food. But the holy man was really Ravana, an evil demon king, in disguise. He kidnapped Sita and carried her off to his palace in Lanka. He wanted to marry Sita but Sita refused.

Prince Rama

Rama is one of the most popular Hindu gods. Hindus believe that he is the god **Vishnu** in a different form. Vishnu came to Earth several times to save the world from danger. This time he came as a royal prince. Hindus **worship** Rama as a hero. He was brave and wise, and loved Sita very much.

Rama and Sita (centre and right) and Lakshman (left).

Rama to the rescue

Hanuman, the monkey general, who helped Rama to rescue Sita.

Rama and Lakshman searched for Sita in the forest. But they could not find her. Then a bird told Rama where Sita was. Hanuman, the monkey general, offered to help Rama. He gathered a huge army together, and set off to the palace in Lanka to rescue Sita. Ravana was furious. He sent his own army of giants and demons to fight them off. A terrible battle raged.

Finally, Rama met Ravana in battle. He killed Ravana with a golden bow and arrow, given to him by the gods. Then he and Sita were reunited. By now, fourteen years had passed and Rama and Sita could go home. People lit lamps to show them the way and to show how good had won over evil. Today, at Divali, **Hindus** still light lamps to welcome Rama and Sita home.

The *Ramayana*

The story of Rama and Sita is told in a long poem called the *Ramayana*. It is one of the Hindus' **holy** books. Hindu children can read the story in comic books and watch it on video or on television.

Children acting out the story of Rama and Sita.

Divali celebrations

Hindus celebrating Divali in the mandir.

In India, Divali lasts for up to five days. It is holiday time for everyone. In Britain, **Hindus** celebrate Divali on the nearest weekend. Many Hindus visit the **mandir** to celebrate with their families and friends. They make offerings of food and flowers to the **deities**. They believe that this is a way of showing and **worshipping** God. In return, they receive God's blessing. This is called **puja**. There is a special puja at Divali weekend.

Divali is also a time for having fun. After the puja, there is music and dancing. The stick dance is very popular. Each dancer has a pair of sticks. They dance around each other, tapping each other's sticks in time to the music. The faster the music, the faster you bang your sticks. You have to mind your fingers! In another dance, dancers hold a **diva** in their hands. But the day is not over yet. There is still the grand firework display to come.

Stick dancing at Divali.

Good fortune

Divali is also the time when **Hindus** remember the goddess **Lakshmi**. She is **Vishnu**'s wife and the goddess of wealth and good fortune. People light **divas** to welcome Lakshmi into their homes. They hope that she will bring them good luck in the year to come. Some people clean their homes from top to bottom, ready for Lakshmi to bless them.

Lakshmi, the goddess of wealth and good luck.

Divali is an important time for Hindu business people. This is when they close their old **account book** and open a new one. They bring their account books to the **mandir** and place a pile of coins on top. Then they perform a special **puja** to Lakshmi. They ask her to bring them good fortune in the new year.

An accounting ceremony at Divali.

Divali cards

Many Hindus send Divali cards to each other. Try making your own. Decorate it with a picture of Lakshmi or some divas. Write 'Happy Divali' inside the card.

Lights and patterns

Divali gets its name from the word *Deepavali* which means 'rows of lights'. Traditionally, people light small clay lamps, filled with oil. These lamps are called **divas**. In Britain, some people put strings of fairy lights around their windows. Lights are also put up in some streets. The lights are for welcoming **Lakshmi** and celebrating Rama and Sita coming home. They also show how good always drives evil away, just as the light drives away darkness.

Diva lights and Divali food.

At Divali, people draw colourful patterns on the doorsteps of their houses. This is to welcome in Lakshmi. These patterns are called rangoli. People use coloured chalk, sand, flour and rice. A favourite pattern for Divali is the **lotus flower** because it is a sign of Lakshmi. In Britain, some **mandirs** hold a rangoli competition for children. The best design wins a prize.

A rangoli pattern.

Divali patterns

Draw your own rangoli pattern with a flower shape in the centre. Use coloured paper and paints. Decorate it with a sprinkle of glitter, coloured sand, rice or lentils.

Food and clothes

Divali is a festival for sharing with family and friends. Many **Hindus** give each other presents. Sometimes this is a piece of silver or gold jewellery. Sometimes it is a set of new clothes. This is a reminder that Divali brings a new year and a time of new beginnings.

At Divali, Hindus eat special food. They may have a Divali meal at home or in the **mandir**. People give boxes of sweets to their friends and relatives. Indian sweets are made of milk products, coconut, nuts and sugar. They are very sweet indeed! People make sweets at home or buy them from sweet-shops.

Indian sweets for Divali.

A girl dressed in her new Divali clothes.

The last day of Divali is called Bhaiya Dooj. It is a time for brothers to visit their sisters' homes. Here they are treated to a delicious meal. In return, the brother promises to look after his sister. He gives her some money, jewellery or clothes as a sign of his love and support. A story explains how this custom began. Long ago, Yama, the angel of death, visited his sister on this day and ate a special meal. He ordered everyone to do the same.

Sikh Divali

Divali is also an important festival for **Sikhs**. This is the time when they remember one of their great teachers, **Guru** Hargobind. He lived in India about 400 years ago. The **emperor** put Guru Hargobind in prison, together with 52 **Hindu** princes. The time came for the Guru to be set free. But he would leave only if all the Hindu princes were allowed to go with him. The emperor agreed.

A Sikh woman lighting a diva.

At Divali, Sikhs celebrate Guru Hargobind's release from prison. They light candles and lamps to welcome the Guru home. Many Sikhs visit the **gurdwara** to **worship**. They remember how Guru Hargobind showed Sikhs that when all peaceful efforts fail, they need to fight to protect what they believe in. Afterwards, they share a meal. The day ends with a firework display.

In India, Harimandir Sahib (the Golden Temple) in Amritsar is lit up with rows of twinkling lights. People float candles in the lake around the temple. It is a very important **shrine** for Sikhs. Amritsar was Guru Hargobind's home.

The Golden Temple at Amritsar.

Around the world

Hindus all over the world celebrate Divali. Most Hindus live in India. There, Divali celebrations can last for five whole days. On the first evening, people light a single lamp for Yama, the angel of death. An image of **Lakshmi** is washed in milk. On the second day, people get up early and eat a special breakfast. They remember the story of how **Krishna** killed a terrible demon called Narakasur and released the princesses he had captured. The third day of Divali is for worshipping Lakshmi. It is also the end of the old year.

Divali fireworks in Bombay, India.

The fourth day of Divali is a time for new starts. It is a day filled with hope for the future. People give gifts of new clothes and jewellery. They remember the story of Rama and how he rescued Sita from wicked Ravana. **Divas** are lit and there are lots of fireworks. In Britain, Hindus also remember these stories in their celebrations.

The last day is Brother's Day. This is when brothers visit their sisters to enjoy a sumptuous feast. Then Divali is over, for another year.

Indonesian shadow puppets are used to tell the story of Rama and Sita.

Hindu festival calendar

January/February	Vasant Panchami/Saraswati Puja (A festival marking the coming of spring and for remembering Saraswati, goddess of art and learning)
February/March	Mahashivratri (A festival for the god Shiva)
February/March	Holi (A festival for remembering Krishna's life and for celebrating spring)
March/April	Ramnavami (Rama's birthday)
March/April	Hanuman Jayanti (Hanuman's birthday)
August	Raksha Bandhan (Sister's and Brother's Day)
August/September	Janmashtami (Krishna's birthday)
August/September	Ganesha Chaturthi (Ganesha's birthday)
September/October	Dassehra/Ma-Durga Puja/Navaratri (Remembers Rama and Sita, and Ma-Durga)
October/November	Divali (The festival of light)

Glossary

account book   book in which business people keep a record of the money they have earned or spent

deity   god or goddess. Hindus believe in a great spirit called Brahman or God. They also worship many deities. Each deity shows a different part of God's power. Avatar is another word for God.

diva   small clay lamp that is lit at Divali

emperor   powerful ruler

gurdwara   place where Sikhs worship

Guru   one of ten great Sikh spiritual teachers

heir   when a king dies, the heir is the person who becomes the next king

Hindu   person who follows the Hindu religion, which began in India thousands of years ago

holy   to do with God or a religious teacher

kingdom   country that is ruled over by a king

Krishna   name of a popular Hindu god

Lakshmi   the goddess of wealth and good fortune

lotus flower   flower that grows in ponds and rivers. It is a special flower for Hindus.

mandir   place where Hindus worship. It is sometimes called a temple.

puja   how Hindus worship. They offer flowers and sweets to the deities and receive God's blessing.

shrine   holy place where deities are worshipped

Sikh   person who follows the Sikh religion, which began in India about 500 years ago

Vishnu   name of a great Hindu god. He protects the world from harm.

worship   to show respect and love to God

Index

Titles in the *Celebrations* series include:

Hardback   0 431 13796 X

Hardback   0 431 13790 0

Hardback   0 431 13793 5

Hardback   0 431 13791 9

Hardback   0 431 13794 3

Hardback   0 431 13795 1

Hardback   0 431 13792 7

Find out about the other titles in this series on our website www.heinemann.co.uk/library